For Love of Lavender

The Culinary Lavender Cookbook

of Delicious Desserts
& Luscious Drinks

For Love of Lavender

The Culinary Lavender Cookbook

of Delicious Desserts
& Luscious Drinks

by

Sunny Savina
the Hidden Alchemist

CHATWIN BOOKS
Seattle, 2015

Cover and book design by Annie Brulé
Cover photo by Phil Tauran (courtesy of Purple Haze Lavender Farm, Sequim, WA)

Chatwin Books Publishing
www.chatwinbooks.com

The Hidden Alchemist
www.thehiddenalchemist.com

Dear Reader, a note on safety.

Some of the recipes in this book include raw eggs. When eggs are consumed raw, there is always a risk that bacteria may be present. For this reason, always only buy certified salmonella-free eggs from a reliable grocer, storing them in a refrigerator until use. Raw eggs should never be consumed by infants or small children, pregnant women, the elderly, or immune-compromised individuals.

The author and publisher accept no responsibility for any adverse effects that may result from the use or application of the recipes and information within this book.

We will accept all credit for your happiness and enjoyment!

❧ Contents ☙

Really Read This

The Essentials of Cooking with Culinary Lavender

What is Culinary Lavender & How Do You Cook With It?

Lavender is lavender, right? Well, yes. If all you want is something that smells amazing, that is true. All lavender is lavender and it all smells divine.

But if you are going to eat it, then stop right there!

Culinary lavender is a variety in and of itself. If you get good culinary lavender, your baked goods and desserts won't taste of perfume. If you don't, they will end up tasting either like a bottle of perfume, or like soap.

If you've ever had a lavender cocktail, or dessert, that tasted bitter, now you know why!

So, always find the finest culinary lavender (if your vendor doesn't know the difference...run away!). If in doubt, pop a blossom in your mouth—it should taste tangy-sweet, but in no way like perfume.

Then, with the right lavender in your pantry, you can begin baking and infusing to the delight of your taste buds.

So now that we've cleared that up...let me tempt you....

The Basics: Essential Principles of Cooking & Baking with Culinary Lavender

The secret to cooking & baking with lavender, is to infuse the flavor into a medium you can bake with—like butter, oil, milk or water.

Once you've infused the flavor into an ingredient, you can use it in your recipes. The difficulty comes from knowing how much (or how little) lavender to use, based on the recipe.

Too much lavender, and the flavor overwhelms; too little, and the flavor is lost in the food.

It is also important to remember that *the more heat and processing you subject the flower to* (whether by blending or baking or infusion), *the stronger the flavor will be.*

If in doubt, use less. Lavender has a strong flavor, and it can become almost bitter if overused. A little goes a long way, so easy does it!

To begin, I will explain how you can create some of the ingredients using the *Infusion Method* for milk, water & butter.

INFUSION is the process of using heat to transfer the flavor, color, and medicinal properties of a plant into another medium, such as water, milk, butter, or oil. For example, tea is an infusion of the tea plant in water.

Syrups & Infusions of Milk, Water, & Butter

*These are the bases from which you build
the delicious recipes to follow. Keep these on hand
and your options will be endless....*

Milk Infusion:

You will need:

- Small saucepan with lid
- Cheesecloth & strainer
- Airtight container
- 1 cup (240ml) of milk of your choice

A word on milk—I've tried this with almond, rice, hemp, coconut & dairy milk. The only recommendation I have is to look for unflavored milks, as the sweetened or flavored variety can cover up the lavender. Also, coconut milk will leave a strong taste of coconut—if you want more of the lavender flavor, make a stronger infusion and use more blossoms!

1. Warm your choice of milk over medium-low heat in a small saucepan, stirring, until it begins to steam
2. Remove immediately from heat, and stir in culinary lavender
3. Allow to steep, covered, for 10-15 minutes
4. Strain well, and store in the refrigerator 1-2 days

Water Infusion:

You will need:

- A very small saucepan (for the stovetop), or a 2 cup glass measuring cup (for the microwave)
- 1 cup (240ml) water
- 1-2 tablespoons (15-30ml) Culinary Lavender
- cheesecloth & strainer
- airtight container (for storage)

1. In small saucepan, bring the water to a boil.
2. Add your dried Culinary Lavender.
3. Stir the lavender until it is thoroughly soaked.
4. Cover the pot and remove from the heat.
5. Allow to steep, until the lavender blossoms sink to the bottom of the sauce pan
6. Strain out the blossoms using your cheesecloth lined strainer.
7. Your infusion should be dark purple.
8. Store in a very clean, airtight container, up to 2 days in the refrigerator

Butter Infusion:

You will need:

- Small saucepan
- 2 sticks (1cup – 240ml) of pure butter (do NOT use margarine for this recipe)
- 2 tablespoons (30ml) of Culinary Lavender
- strainer & cheesecloth
- glass or ceramic bowl

1. Melt the butter in a small saucepan over very low heat.

2. Stir the lavender blossoms into the butter. (Alternately, you can put the lavender into a small bundle of cheesecloth and immerse the bundle).

3. Continue to warm the butter & lavender over low heat for 5 minutes, stirring.

4. Remove from heat and cover with a towel, or a bit of cloth.

5. Allow to sit until the butter has re-solidified (or overnight).

6. Return to heat, and melt again.

7. Once melted, strain out the lavender blossoms, using cheesecloth layered over a strainer, to clarify the butter.

8. If desired, you can wait for the butter to become semi-solid, and whip with a hand mixer creating delicious Whipped Lavender Butter—excellent on scones!

Store in airtight container in the refrigerator, up to 1 week.

Lavender Simple Syrup

You will need:

- Small saucepan with lid
- 1 cup (240 ml) water
- 2 cups (480 ml) sugar (I use evaporated cane juice, which is a more ethically produced sugar)
- Cheesecloth & strainer
- Candy thermometer
- Airtight container—I also highly recommend using a funnel if your airtight container has a narrow neck. This stuff is HOT folks.

Make 1 cup **Lavender Water Infusion** (see above).

1. Strain using cheesecloth & a strainer to remove every last bit of lavender blossoms

2. Reheat your infusion back to boiling over high heat (this is easier if you keep your saucepan covered, most of the time)

3. After your infusion is boiling, gradually stir in your sugar until it is completely dissolved. The mixture should be dark, dark purple, and the surface of the syrup should look glossy

4. Bring the mixture back up to a gentle boil, ideally to 200°

5. Remove from heat

IMPORTANT: *do not allow the mixture to get too hot after you add the sugar—at 300° you end up with candy!*

Pour into a completely clean glass container. Allow to cool, and cover. May be stored in the refrigerator for 2 weeks.

Some suggestions for your Simple Syrup?

 Iced Tea • Coffee • Ginger Ale
Italian Sodas • Martinis • Lemonade

Five Minute Desserts

Don't have much time? *If you have some Lavender Syrup on hand, a fast but delicious dessert is ready in minutes!*

Lavender Glaze or Whipped Cream create a quick and easy dessert out of almost anything.

Glaze:

You will need:

- 2-3 Tablespoons (30-45ml) of confectioner's sugar
- 1 Tablespoon (15ml) of **Lavender Syrup**
- Whisk & small bowl

1. Spoon confectioners sugar into a small bowl.
2. Add the **Lavender Syrup** to the sugar, and blend with a small whisk or fork. If the glaze is too thin for your purposes, add a little sugar. If too thick, add syrup.
3. Glaze your favorite dessert, cookie or breakfast! This works especially well on shortbread & biscotti.

   My *favorite* is drizzling this over gelato!

Whipped Cream:

You will need:

- ½ cup (120ml) of heavy whipping cream
- 1 tablespoon (15ml) of **Lavender Syrup**
- Tall bowl

With a hand mixer or immersion blender, whip the heavy cream with syrup until fluffy and light.

Try your Whipped Cream or Glaze on:

Shortbread • Pancakes • Sugar Cookies
Biscotti • Lemon Bars • Waffles
Ice Cream • Crepes
Mini Doughnuts

Quick Desserts

These can be made with just a little bit of prep time, plus the time it takes to bake.

Lavender Pound Cake

You will need:

- 1 cup (240ml) softened butter (easiest way to do this is to set your butter out on the counter overnight in a covered container)
- 2 cups (480ml) sugar
- 4 room temperature eggs
- 3 tablespoons (45ml) **Lavender Syrup**
- 2 cups (480 ml) flour
- Large bowl & wooden spoon
- Hand mixer (it gets super difficult without one, unless you are a body-builder or something!)
- Loaf pan, with the bottom greased with butter

Heat oven to 375°.

1. In large bowl, beat your soft butter with a hand mixer until it is smooth.
2. In this order, add and beat in ingredients:
   First – 2 cups sugar (until smooth)
   Second – 4 room temperature eggs
   Third – 3 tablespoons syrup
   Fourth – 2 cups flour
3. *At this point, the mixture should be extremely thick*
4. Pour (or scoop!) into your non-stick loaf pan, with a greased bottom. At this point, I like to sprinkle lavender blossoms on top, but that is optional!

Bake 35-45 minutes. A stick inserted in the center should come out clean.

Cool on a wire rack, 10 minutes, and remove from pan.

I love to serve my pound cake with my **Lavender Glaze**!

Lavender Brownies

You will need:

- 4 large room temperature eggs
- ½ cup (120ml) butter
- 4oz (120g) semi-sweet chocolate
- ½ tsp salt
- 1 cup (240ml) flour
- 2 cups (480ml) sugar
- medium bowl
- small saucepan
- wooden spoon & spatula
- 9" x 9" non-stick pan

Pre-heat your oven to 350°

1. Melt your butter (**Lavender Butter** will add more flavor!) and your semi-sweet chocolate squares in a small pan over very low heat (or in the microwave, stirring every 15 seconds).

2. Set this aside—and allow it to cool! This is an important step. If you are rushed, set it in the refrigerator for 10 minutes. It should be no more than warm when you use it.

3. In a separate bowl, beat your 4 room temperature eggs until they are light and foamy, adding your salt a bit at a time. Gradually beat in your sugar and syrup.

4. Now...Put. Away. Your. Mixer. Seriously, do the rest by hand.

5. With your wooden spoon, gently mix in the cooled chocolate & butter mixture.

6. After it is combined, gently fold in, a few spoonfuls at a time, the flour.

7. It is very important you do not over-mix this, or your brownies won't be light and fluffy. Once the flour is mixed in, STOP MIXING.

8. Grease only the bottom of your pan with a bit of butter, and pour the batter into the pan.

Bake for 40-45 minutes at 350°.

Serve when cool—this is great with **Lavender Whipped Cream**, by the way.

Lavender Griddle Cakes

You will need:

- ¾ cup (180ml) flour
- 1 teaspoon (5ml) salt
- 1 teaspoon (5ml) baking powder
- 2 tablespoons (30ml) powdered sugar
- 2 large room temperature eggs
- 2/3 cup milk (use **Lavender Milk Infusion** for a stronger flavor)
- 1/3 cup **Lavender Water Infusion**
- Mixing bowls & a whisk
- Flat griddle & oil or butter
- A sifter

1. Sift together your flour, salt, baking powder & powdered sugar
2. In a separate bowl, beat your eggs until light & fluffy, and then add your milk and lavender infusion.

3. Make a "well" (indentation) in your sifted dry ingredients, pour the liquid ingredients into the well, and combine them with as few strokes as possible (try not to over mix, and don't worry about getting out every little lump)

4. If your mixture is too thick, add milk a teaspoon at a time, until the correct consistency is achieved. The mixture should flow off the spoon easily, but not be watery.

5. Heat a flat skillet, or non-stick pan, and drop in a small amount of butter to grease the pan. Pour a small quantity of batter, and allow it to spread. The pancakes should be about 3-5" across, depending on your preference.

When the cake is browned on one side, turn it over to brown it on the other.

Makes approximately 16 four-inch griddle cakes.

I love to serve these topped with **Lavender Whipped Cream** & filled with blueberries!

Not So Quick Desserts

These take a little longer to prepare, but are well worth the trouble.... All are about half an hour of preparation, plus baking time.

Lavender Meringue Pie

You will need:

- A pie shell – either purchased or made by hand.
  If you bake a pie shell, it should be thoroughly cooled.
- A small saucepan
- 1 cup (240ml) sugar
- 5 tablespoons arrowroot (or cornstarch)
- Pinch of salt
- 1 cup (240ml) **Lavender Infusion**
- 1 cup (240ml) Milk or **Lavender Milk** for a stronger flavor
- 3 egg yolks *(reserve the whites if you will be making meringue)*
- 3 tablespoons (45ml) butter (do not use margarine)
- 2 tablespoons (30ml) **Lavender Syrup**
- Mixing bowls, whisk & spoon
- Hand Mixer & spatulas

Heat oven to 350°. Purchase or make a pie shell.
If you bake a pie shell, it should be thoroughly cooled.

1. Sift together into your small saucepan: sugar, arrowroot or cornstarch, salt.
2. Add very gradually: your **Lavender Water Infusion** & milk.
3. Stir and cook these ingredients over medium heat until it thickens (about 10 minutes), stirring occasionally.

4. Cover and cook over low heat for 10 minutes more.

5. In a small bowl, beat 3 egg yolks *(reserving your egg whites for the meringue—see next page)*.

6. In a separate bowl, pour 3 teaspoons *(one teaspoon at a time)*, of the hot mixture over the eggs, beating with a whisk.

7. Pour the egg mixture back into the saucepan, and mix, stirring and cooking over low heat, about 5 minutes more.

8. Remove from heat and pour into medium bowl. Beat in your butter and **Lavender Syrup.**

9. Make Meringue (below).

Lavender Meringue:

1. Whip 3 egg whites until stiff. They should stand in peaks that fall over when the beater is removed.

2. Beat in, ½ tsp. at a time, 3 Tablespoons sugar and 1 Tablespoon **Lavender Syrup.** Do not overbeat.

To complete the recipe:

• Pour the custard into a cool pie shell.

• Cover custard with meringue

• Bake 10-15 minutes, remove from oven, and cool.

Lavender Pineapple Upside Down Cake

You will need:

- An oven-safe skillet, or glass cake pan
- 2 tablespoons (30ml) butter (or **Lavender Butter**)
- 1 tablespoon (15ml) culinary lavender
- 2 tablespoons (30ml) **Lavender Syrup**
- Pineapple slices (about 5-6 rings)
- Reserved pineapple juice (6 tablespoons)
- 2 eggs
- ½ cup sugar (120ml)
- 1 cup flour (240ml)
- 1/3 tsp (10ml) baking powder
- Mixing bowls & spoons
- Hand mixer or whisk

Heat the oven to 350°.

1. In non-stick, oven safe skillet, melt the butter (either on the stove, or by putting your pan in the warming oven).
2. Sprinkle the lavender blossoms into the melted butter.

3. Arrange pineapple slices in the melted butter.

4. Drizzle the Lavender Syrup over the pineapple slices

5. Set aside.

6. In a medium bowl, beat the eggs, sugar & pineapple juice until smooth

7. Sift in your flour and baking powder & mix well.

8. Pour batter over pineapple slices in your skillet.

Bake for 45 minutes at 350°.
A wooden pick inserted in the center of the cake should come out clean.

9. When done, remove from the oven.

10. Immediately turn cake over onto a flat serving plate.

11. Wait to remove the pan for a few moments, to allow the cake to separate completely from the pan.

Serve warm, with plain or **Lavender Whipped Cream.**

Lavender Cheesecake

All ingredients should be at room temperature.
"Fat Free" varieties of cream cheese should **not** be used.
I find that brown eggs just work better. But feel free to use white
   eggs if you want.

You will need:

- 8" springform pan
- 3 graham crackers
- butter (for the pan)
- optional: Culinary Lavender blossoms
- 24oz cream cheese
- 4 large brown eggs, room temperature
- 1 cup (240ml) sugar
- 3 tablespoons (45ml) **Lavender Syrup**
- mixing bowls and hand mixer

set aside for Topping (opposite page):

- 8oz of sour cream
- 1 tablespoon of **Lavender Syrup**

Heat oven to 350°.

CHEESECAKE:

1. Butter the sides and bottom (thickly) of your springform pan.

2. Thoroughly crush 3 graham crackers until they are powdered.

3. Roll them in the buttered pan, until the sides and bottom are coated with crumbs.

4. Allow any remaining crumbs to settle on the bottom.

5. Optional: I like to sprinkle a spoonful of lavender blossoms onto the crust at this point as well.

6. In a large bowl, beat the room temperature cream cheese, until it is smooth.

7. In a separate bowl, whip your egg whites until very stiff.

8. Gradually beat in the sugar, a bit at a time, to create a meringue.

9. Slowly add the meringue to the cream cheese, and beat with a mixer, until smooth

10. Add the **Lavender Syrup**, and continue to beat, until everything is blended.

11. Gently spoon the cheese mixture into the pan. It should be quite thick, needing to be spread out with a spoon.

Bake at 325° degrees for 30 minutes. Remove from the oven.

TOPPING:

1. Whip the thick sour cream with **Lavender Syrup**.

2. Gently spoon this mixture over hot cheesecake.

3. Increase the heat of your oven to 475°.

4. Return topped cake to oven for 10 minutes.

5. Remove from the oven and allow to cool slowly to room temperature (I usually put it on top of the stove to slow the process).

Serve chilled.

Lavender Shortbread

You will need:

- 1 ½ cup **Lavender Butter** (see above recipe)
- 2/3 cup sugar
- ¼ cup confectioners sugar
- 1 teaspoon grated lemon zest
- 2 ½ cup flour
- ½ cup potato or corn starch
- ¼ teaspoon salt
- 1 tablespoon Culinary Lavender
- 2 mixing bowls
- cookie sheet
- wire cooling racks
- spoon & spatula & whisk

1. In medium bowl, cream butter, white sugar, & confectioners sugar until light and fluffy.
2. Add in lemon zest & Culinary Lavender.
3. Combine, in separate bowl, flour, starch & salt.
4. Gradually mix into butter & sugar mixture until well blended

5. Divide dough into two balls, flatten until 1" thick, and cover with plastic wrap

6. Refrigerate until firm (about 1 hour)

Preheat oven to 325°

7. On a lightly floured surface, roll dough to ¼" thick & cut into shapes

8. Place on your cookie sheet & bake for 18-20 minutes until cookies brown at the edges.

9. Cool on wire racks

Glaze:

• 1 tablespoon Lavender Syrup
• 2 tablespoons confectioner's sugar

1. Mix together with whisk.

2. Dip or pour over shortbread

3. Wait 5 minutes for the glaze to harden (or put in the fridge for a few minutes).

Lavender Tapioca

You will need:

- 3 cups whole dairy milk or whole coconut milk (don't use skim milk for this one!)
- ½ cup quick cooking tapioca
- ½ cup white sugar
- ¼ teaspoon salt
- 2 eggs, beaten
- 3 tablespoons culinary lavender
- small saucepan
- small bowl
- whisk & spoons

1. Warm the milk in saucepan until steaming, add the lavender blossoms, reduce the heat and simmer for 10 minutes, and strain

2. Add tapioca to the warmed milk, add sugar & salt

3. Slowly bring to a boil over medium heat, stirring constantly to prevent scorching the milk.

4. Reduce the heat to the lowest setting, and cook—stirring— for 5 minutes more.

5. Whisk one cup of the hot milk into the beaten eggs, *a Tablespoon or two at a time,* until the entire cup of milk is mixed

6. Pour the egg & milk mixture back into the tapioca and stir until well mixed

7. Bring your pudding to a gentle simmer over medium-low heat.

8. Cook & stir 2 minutes longer, until pudding is thick enough to evenly coat the back of your spoon.

9. Remove from heat

10. For extra flavor, you can stir in 2 Tablespoons of **Lavender Syrup**

11. Serve hot, or pour into ramekins & chill

Drinks

Lavender Hibiscus Lemonade

You will need:

- 3 cups water + another 3 cups water (total 6 cups)
- 1 ½ cup lemon juice
- 1 ¼ cup white sugar or cane juice
- 2 Tablespoons Culinary Lavender
- 2 teaspoons hibiscus blossoms
- pitcher
- small saucepan
- funnel
- strainer
- spoon

1. In your pitcher, mix 3 cups water and the lemon juice, chill
2. Bring remaining 3 cups of water to a boil in your sauce pan
3. Add lavender & hibiscus to boiling water.
4. Remove from heat & allow to steep in the hot water for 10-15 minutes
5. Strain out the blossoms. You now have Lavender Simple Syrup.
6. Bring the water back to a boil, and add the sugar, stirring until it returns to a boil
7. Remove from heat & allow to cool (for more rapid cooling, place the pan in a shallow basin of cold water, making sure the water doesn't get into the pan!)
8. Add cooled Lavender Simple Syrup to the lemon water, and enjoy!

Lavender Horchata

Pronounced....*oar-CHA-ta*...a Mexican drink that is creamy and deliciously satisfying.

You will need:

- 2 cups white rice (I prefer sweet rice, but any white rice will do)
- 4 cups water
- 2 cups **Lavender Water Infusion**
- 2 cups Lavender **Milk Infusion** (any milk will work, but increase the water to 7 cups if you use coconut milk with cream)
- 4 tablespoons **Lavender Syrup**
- mixing bowls
- pitcher
- spoon
- blender or hand mixer

1. Take your 4 cups water, and place into a bowl with the rice.
2. Blend with a hand mixer (or blend in the blender)
3. Allow the rice and water to soak for at least an hour—many say you must soak the rice overnight, but I could never taste any difference
4. Strain out the rice
5. Blend your remaining ingredients—**Lavender Water and Milk Infusions** and syrup into a pitcher
6. Chill & serve over ice
7. Stir regularly, as the ingredients tend to settle

*Please visit the shop
for more delicious lavender creations....*

THE HIDDEN ALCHEMIST
214 1st Ave. S., Suite B1
Seattle, WA 98104

www.thehiddenalchemist.com
206.802.8236

The Hidden Alchemist

What is an Alchemist, you might ask? Well, alchemy is the word we used before we used the word chemistry (get it? *al-chemia*). In past centuries, an alchemist could be studying the planets, or she could be an herbalist, or he could be trying to figure out how to turn iron into gold…but it meant, at its root, a person who was devoted to learning all there was to learn about the natural or supernatural world, through experimentation, and science.

Nowadays, nobody really remembers much about the meaning of being an alchemist. But in my life, I am an herbalist, and I study the natural world, and I blend science and history, old wives' tales and scientific journals.

It has become my life: helping people use plants, and the tools nature placed all around us.

However, I discovered that having fun is just as important, and so I began creating recipes for culinary lavender. And let me tell you, watching the smile of sheer delight come over someone's face when tasting my syrup for the first time has just as much healing joy as getting rid of a headache!

So…I am the Alchemist, or Herbalist, or Healer, or Cook—use whatever word means something to you. The label isn't nearly as important as the meaning.

Taste a bit of summer in my recipes, and smile.

Sunny Savina
Owner, The Hidden Alchemist
Pioneer Square, Seattle

Sunny Savina

Sunny has been an Herbalist, Alchemist or Mad Scientist (depending on your point of view) for about 20 years now. Currently, she is devoting random swathes of 80 hours per week to her very first Apothecary & Tea Shop (The Hidden Alchemist), in addition to taking care of a husband, a pet snake named Sally The Escape Artist and a pet cat known as The Queen of he Known Universe, or Your Majesty for short.

In her spare time, Sunny loves to zoom around Pioneer Square on a scooter named "Sugar," make monthly forays to the Olympic Mountains in order to pick up fresh herbs from the farm, go for long horseback rides in search of elusive botanicals, and try to convince her horse Goldie that the one with four legs is never the one in charge.

Sunny's future plans include writing a couple books on practical Herbalism, and getting some sleep…really, really soon.

CPSIA information can be obtained at www.ICGtesting.com
Printed in the USA
LVOW07s2246140715

446243LV00002B/4/P